T0127451

GARLIC

GARLIC
A BOOK OF RECIPES

HELEN SUDELL

LORENZ BOOKS

First published in 2013 by Lorenz Books
an imprint of Anness Publishing Limited
Blaby Road, Wigston, Leicestershire LE18 4SE
www.annesspublishing.com
www.lorenzbooks.com
info@anness.com

If you like the images in this book and would like to investigate
using them for publishing, promotions or advertising, please visit
our website www.practicalpictures.com for more information

A CIP catalogue record for this book is available from
The British Library

Publisher Joanna Lorenz
Editorial Director Helen Sudell
Designer Nigel Partridge
Illustrations Anna Koska

Photographers: Martin Brigdale, Nicki Dowey, Michelle Garrett,
William Lingwood, Thomas Odulate, Craig Robertson, Jon Whitaker
Recipes by: Ghillie Basan, Kate Whiteman, Brian Glover, Judy
Bastyra, Jenny White, Joanna Farrow, Pepita Aris, Marlena Spieler,
Carol Wilson, Ewa Michalik, Maxine Clark, Rena Salaman,
Christine Ingram

Printed and bound in China

COOK'S NOTES

• Bracketed terms are intended for American readers.

• For all recipes, quantities are given in both metric and imperial
measures and, where appropriate, in standard cups and spoons.
Follow one set of measures, but not a mixture, because they are
not interchangeable.

• Standard spoon and cup measures are level. 1 tsp = 5ml, 1 tbsp =
15ml, 1 cup = 250ml/8fl oz.

• Australian standard tablespoons are 20ml. Australian readers
should use 3 tsp in place of 1 tbsp for measuring small quantities.

• American pints are 16fl oz/2 cups. American readers should use
20fl oz/2.5 cups in place of 1 pint when measuring liquids.

• Electric oven temperatures in this book are for conventional
ovens. When using a fan oven, the temperature will probably need
to be reduced by about 10–20°C/20–40°F. Since ovens vary, you
should check with your manufacturer's instruction book for
guidance.

• The nutritional analysis given for each recipe is calculated per
portion (i.e. serving or item), unless otherwise stated. If the recipe
gives a range, such as Serves 4–6, then the nutritional analysis will
be for the smaller portion size, i.e. 6 servings. The analysis does not
include optional ingredients, such as salt added to taste.

• Medium (US large) eggs are used unless otherwise stated.

PUBLISHER'S NOTE

CONTENTS

INTRODUCTION

Garlic (*Allium sativum*) has been grown for centuries and is inextricably linked with folklore, medicine and rugged country cooking. It evokes strong feelings because of its distinctive aroma, however it is regarded as one of the finest culinary herbs, with its unique ability to add intense or subtle flavour.

There are many different varieties of garlic, most of them geographically specific and therefore adapted to local

Below: Crushing garlic with salt will help release its aroma.

climate and conditions. Garlic stores well when it is dried, but has a different taste from when it is used green and freshly pulled. There are some garlics with very white skin, while others are stained or mottled with an attractive deep pink skin colour.

COOKING WITH GARLIC

Garlic is an almost universal favourite ingredient for cuisines all around the world. It is widely used, both raw and cooked, to flavour all kinds of dishes. It is used raw in dressings, salsas, butters and salads. Cooked, it is used in huge quantities in most Asian countries, Mexico and South America, the Middle East and in all Mediterranean countries, often mixed with herbs and other spices.

Garlic alters in flavour according to how it is prepared and for how long it is cooked. Crushed garlic, either raw or

Above: Garlic is considered by many to be the most important culinary ingredient.

briefly cooked, is the most pungent and strongly flavoured; a whole head of garlic, slowly roasted until it becomes purée soft will have a mellow, nutty, toasty flavour and can be eaten in its entirety. Garlic may be fried, baked, roasted or braised. It is a ubiquitous ingredient in most spice pastes, Spanish salsas, Italian pestos and Mexican moles. It is also widely used in all types of cuisine in marinades, soups and stews.

GROWING AND HARVESTING GARLIC

Garlic is grown from individual cloves in a similar way to onion and shallot sets. There are many different varieties of garlic and it is better to order an appropriate variety from a seed firm, rather than using a head of garlic from the supermarket. Garlic needs a long growing season and also a period of 1–2 months of cold weather (0–10°C/ 32–50°F) to make a good-size head.

Garlic is different from other alliums in that the head, or

Below: For the best results, plant garlic cloves in the autumn.

bulb, grows underground rather than on the surface of the soil. Because of this, garlic is best planted in the autumn, to be harvested in mid- to late summer the following year. It will tolerate some frost. Little or no growth will be visible above ground until the following spring.

Plant individual cloves 10–15cm/4–6in apart in straight rows 25cm/10in apart just below the surface in well-dug soil. Place a little sand beneath each clove if gardening on heavy, clay soil to help drainage and prevent rotting.

When the leaves begin to die back, wither and keel over in mid to late summer, the garlic is ready to be harvested. In a period of dry weather gently pull up the garlic bulbs, brush off any excess soil and leave them to dry out for a few days.

STORING GARLIC

Garlic is best stored hung up in a dry, well-ventilated room or shed that is cool and just frost-

Above: Stringing garlic is an excellent way of ensuring that it stays dry, and if hung in a well-ventilated room garlic will keep fresh for longer.

free. Garlic can be strung together to form ropes or skeins, either by plaiting the stalks together or tying them together with string or raffia. An alternative method of 'stringing' garlic is simply to thread a stiff wire through the dry necks of the bulb, make a hook at the end and hang up.

TYPES OF GARLIC

Garlic is used in many different cuisines and is now available in a variety of forms.

WHITE GARLIC
This variety of garlic has a white papery, silky skin. A single bulb consists on average of 8 to 10 plump cloves.

PURPLE GARLIC
Considered by many to have a superior flavour. The skin may be pink, violet or purple.

ELEPHANT GARLIC
A large variety which is the mildest of all and can be cooked as a vegetable.

SMOKED GARLIC
Whole heads of garlic are hot-smoked so that they are partly cooked and infused with wood smoke. It adds a delicate smoked flavour to fish and chicken dishes.

PICKLED GARLIC
Available in delicatessens and some specialist shops, this comes in jars of either whole bulbs or separate cloves. It is very pungent, and easy to make at home.

GARLIC PEPPER AND SALT
These products, as their name implies, combine garlic with seasoning. Use in dressings, casseroles or salads.

Left: Pickled garlic is a popular flavouring in Thai food.

GARLIC PUREE
Convenient if fresh garlic is not to hand, but the flavour is not comparable.

FROZEN GARLIC
Another convenient form of garlic, pre-chopped and frozen. Again not really comparable to fresh garlic.

DRIED GARLIC
Available minced, chopped, powdered and in granules. In its dehydrated form, it is almost odourless, but when rehydrated the flavour is good. These forms of garlic are useful for adding to sauces, curries, soups, stews, salads, chutneys and pickles.

GARLIC BREAD SEASONING
A useful seasoning to make quick garlic butter, which can be spread on French bread before baking. Garlic butter can also be melted over hot, cooked vegetables, grilled meat and steamed fish.

White garlic

Garlic bread seasoning

Frozen garlic

Garlic salt

Garlic pickle

Minced garlic

Pickled garlic

Smoked garlic

Garlic powder

Elephant garlic

Garlic cloves

Garlic purée

Garlic pepper

Dried chopped garlic

Garlic granules

Purple garlic

Pickled whole garlic

BASIC TECHNIQUES AND RECIPES

All you really need to prepare garlic are a good, small, sharp knife and a chopping board.

PEELING AND CHOPPING GARLIC

Separate the cloves from the main bulb or pull single cloves from the bulb as required.

1 To peel, lay a large knife on top of the garlic and bang it gently to loosen the skin. Crush the peeled clove with the side of the knife to flatten it. Chop the garlic finely by holding the tip of the knife on the board and lifting only the handle end, moving the blade across the clove. Garlic can be crushed in a garlic crusher but this tends to give it a harsher flavour.

COOKING WITH GARLIC

Garlic is endlessly versatile and can be blended with butter, steeped in olive oil, or made into a rich purée to be used as needed.

Garlic butter: This can be prepared in advance and then chilled or frozen until required. To freeze, wrap well in clear film (plastic wrap) and then in foil.

1 Place 115g/4oz unsalted butter in a large mixing bowl and beat continuously with a wooden spoon or electric mixer until soft.

2 Add 1–2 chopped garlic cloves and season to taste. Blend together well.

3 Keeping the butter and your hands cool, place the blended butter on a large piece of greaseproof (waxed) paper and shape into a roll. Wrap the roll in the paper and chill until firm. Unwrap it and cut into rounds.

Garlic oil: This oil takes on the delicious flavour of fresh garlic and is invaluable for enlivening salad dressings and sauces, and for sautéeing.

1 Trim the root ends from 6–8 cloves of fresh garlic and peel off the skin. Hold the garlic cloves one at a time between the thumb and finger and, using the back of a heavy knife near the handle, crush the cloves by pressing down heavily onto a chopping board.

2 Place all the crushed garlic in a screw-topped jar. Add 120ml/4fl oz/½ cup olive oil and cap. Store the oil for up to 2 weeks in the refrigerator.

Left: Aioli and spicy potato wedges are a great combination.

Roasted garlic purée: This will store for several weeks as long as you keep the purée covered with 1cm/½ in of oil. This recipe makes 120ml/4fl oz/ ½ cup purée.

1 Cut a thin slice off the top of 5 heads of garlic.

2 Wrap the garlic heads in foil with two sprigs of rosemary

and drizzle over 45ml/3 tbsp oil. Bake at 190°C/375°F/Gas 5 for 50–60 minutes, then cool.

3 Squeeze the garlic out of its skin into a bowl, then mash, and beat in 30ml/2 tbsp extra virgin olive oil and season. Spoon into a sterilized jar. Pour over oil to cover by about 1cm/½ in and store in the refrigerator for up to 3 weeks.

Aioli: This rich garlicky mayonnaise is usually served with crudities as a starter.

1 Put 4 crushed garlic cloves in a bowl with a pinch of salt and blend together with the back of a spoon. Add 2 egg yolks and beat with an electric mixer for 30 seconds until creamy.

2 Beat in 250ml/8fl oz/1 cup olive oil: add it drop by drop until the mixture thickens, then add the olive oil in a thin stream. Thin the mayonnaise with a few drops of lemon juice and season to taste. Chill in the refrigerator for up to 2 days.

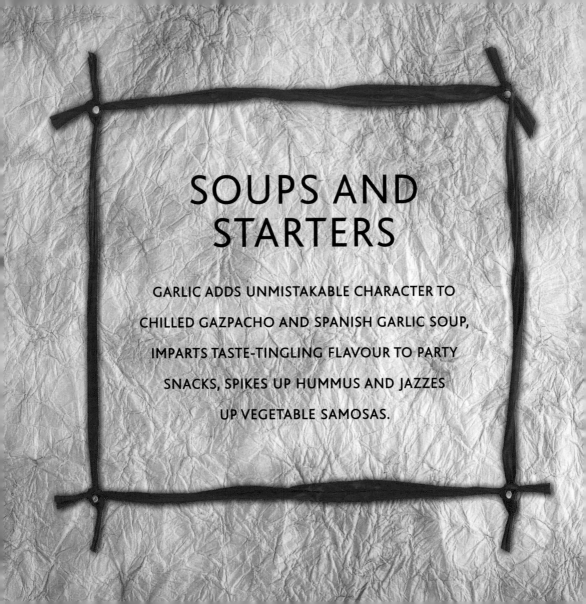

SOUPS AND STARTERS

GARLIC ADDS UNMISTAKABLE CHARACTER TO
CHILLED GAZPACHO AND SPANISH GARLIC SOUP,
IMPARTS TASTE-TINGLING FLAVOUR TO PARTY
SNACKS, SPIKES UP HUMMUS AND JAZZES
UP VEGETABLE SAMOSAS.

SPANISH GARLIC SOUP

This is a simple and satisfying soup, made with one of the most popular ingredients in the Mediterranean – garlic!

Serves 4

30ml/2 tbsp olive oil
4 large garlic cloves, peeled
4 slices French bread, 5mm/¼in
  thick
15ml/1 tbsp paprika
1 litre/1¾ pints/4 cups beef
  stock
1.5ml/¼ tsp ground cumin
pinch of saffron strands
4 eggs
salt and ground black pepper
chopped fresh parsley, to
  garnish

Energy 253kcal/1061kJ; Protein 11.8g;
Carbohydrate 26.5g, of which sugars 1.5g;
Fat 12g, of which saturates 2.5g;
Cholesterol 190mg; Calcium 82mg;
Fibre 2g; Sodium 318mg

Preheat the oven to 230°C/450°F/Gas 8. Heat the oil in a large pan. Add the whole garlic cloves and cook until golden. Remove and set aside. Fry the bread in the oil until golden, then set aside.

Add the paprika to the pan, and fry for a few seconds. Stir in the beef stock, cumin and saffron, then add the reserved garlic, crushing the cloves with the back of a wooden spoon. Season with salt and pepper then cook for about 5 minutes.

Ladle the soup into four ovenproof bowls and break an egg into each. Place the slices of fried bread on top of the egg and place in the oven for about 3–4 minutes, until the eggs are set. Sprinkle with parsley and serve at once.

GAZPACHO

This classic chilled soup is deeply rooted in Andalusia, Spain. The soothing blend of tomatoes, sweet peppers and garlic is sharpened with sherry vinegar, and enriched with olive oil.

Serves 4
1.3–1.6kg/3–3½lb ripe
    tomatoes
1 green (bell) pepper, seeded
    and roughly chopped
2 garlic cloves, finely chopped
2 slices stale bread, crusts
    removed
60ml/4 tbsp extra virgin olive oil
60ml/4 tbsp sherry vinegar
150ml/¼ pint/⅔ cup tomato
    juice
300ml/½ pint/1¼ cups iced
    water
salt and ground black pepper
ice cubes, to serve (optional)

For the garnishes
30ml/2 tbsp olive oil
2–3 slices stale bread, diced
1 small cucumber, peeled and
    finely diced
1 small onion, finely chopped
1 red (bell) and 1 green (bell)
    pepper, seeded and finely
    diced
2 hard-boiled eggs, chopped

Skin the tomatoes, then quarter them and remove the cores and seeds, saving the juices. Put the pepper in a food processor and process for a few seconds. Add the tomatoes, reserved juices, garlic, bread, oil and vinegar and process. Add the tomato juice and blend to combine.

Season the soup, then pour into a large bowl, cover with clear film (plastic wrap) and chill for at least 12 hours.

Prepare the garnishes. Heat the olive oil in a frying pan and fry the bread cubes for 4–5 minutes until golden brown and crisp. Drain well on kitchen paper, then arrange in a small dish. Place each of the remaining garnishes in separate small dishes.

Just before serving, dilute the soup with the ice-cold water. The consistency should be thick but not too stodgy. If you like, stir a few ice cubes into the soup, then spoon into serving bowls and serve with the garnishes.

COOK'S TIP
In Spain, ripe tomatoes are used for salads and very ripe ones for sauces and soups. No further flavouring ingredients are needed. If you cannot find really ripe tomatoes, add a pinch of sugar to sweeten the soup slightly.

Energy 356kcal/1494kJ; Protein 7.6g; Carbohydrate 41.9g, of which sugars 21.5g; Fat 18.8g, of which saturates 2.9g; Cholesterol 0mg; Calcium 90mg; Fibre 6.7g; Sodium 3460mg

ROASTED GARLIC AND GOAT'S CHEESE SOUFFLÉ

The mellow flavour of roasted garlic pervades this simple soufflé. Balance the rich soufflé with a crisp green salad, including peppery leaves, such as mizuna and watercress.

Serves 3–4

2 large heads of garlic
3 fresh thyme sprigs
15ml/1 tbsp olive oil
250ml/8fl oz/1 cup milk
1 fresh bay leaf
2 x 1cm/½in thick onion slices
2 cloves
50g/2oz/¼ cup butter
40g/1½oz/⅓ cup plain (all-purpose) flour
cayenne pepper
3 eggs, separated, plus 1 egg white
150g/5oz goat's cheese, crumbled
50g/2oz/⅔ cup freshly grated Parmesan cheese
2.5–5ml/½–1 tsp chopped fresh thyme
2.5ml/½ tsp cream of tartar
salt and ground black pepper

Energy 563kcal/2338kJ; Protein 28.8g;
Carbohydrate 16.5g, of which sugars
5.8g; Fat 42.9g, of which saturates 24.1g;
Cholesterol 294mg; Calcium 422mg;
Fibre 0.7g; Sodium 710mg.

Preheat the oven to 180°C/350°F/Gas 4. Place the garlic and thyme sprigs on a piece of foil. Sprinkle with the oil and close the foil around the garlic. Bake for about 1 hour, until the garlic is soft. Leave to cool.

Squeeze the garlic out of its skin. Discard the thyme and garlic skins, then purée the garlic flesh with the oil.

Meanwhile, place the milk, bay leaf, onion slices and cloves in a small saucepan. Bring to the boil, then remove from the heat. Cover and leave to stand for 30 minutes.

Melt 40g/1½oz/3 tbsp of the butter in another pan. Stir in the flour and cook gently for 2 minutes, stirring. Reheat and strain the milk, then gradually stir it into the flour and butter.

Cook the sauce very gently for 10 minutes, stirring frequently. Season with salt, pepper and a pinch of cayenne. Cool slightly. Preheat the oven to 200°C/400°F/Gas 6.

Beat in the egg yolks one at a time. Then beat in the goat's cheese, all but 15ml/1 tbsp of the Parmesan and the chopped thyme. Use the remaining butter to grease 1 large soufflé dish or 4 large ramekins .

Whisk the egg whites and cream of tartar in a scrupulously clean bowl until firm, but not dry. Stir 45ml/3 tbsp of the whites into the sauce, then gently, but thoroughly, fold in the remainder.

Pour the mixture into the prepared dish or dishes. Run a knife around the edge of each dish, pushing the mixture away from the rim. Scatter with the reserved Parmesan.

Place the dish or dishes on a baking sheet and cook for 25–30 minutes for a large soufflé or 20 minutes for small soufflés. The mixture should be risen and firm to a light touch in the centre; it should not wobble excessively when given a light push. Serve immediately.

POTATO, SHALLOT AND GARLIC SAMOSAS

Most samosas are deep-fried. These are baked, making them a healthier option. They are also perfect for parties, since the pastries need no last-minute attention.

Makes 25

1 large potato, about 250g/
    9oz, diced
15ml/1 tbsp groundnut
    (peanut) oil
2 shallots, finely chopped
1 garlic clove, finely chopped
60ml/4 tbsp coconut milk
5ml/1 tsp Thai red or green
    curry paste
75g/3oz/¾ cup peas
juice of ½ lime
25 samosa wrappers or 10 x
    5cm/4 x 2in strips of filo
    pastry
salt and ground black pepper
oil, for brushing

COOK'S TIP
Many Asian food stores sell what is described as a samosa pad. This is a packet, usually frozen, containing about 50 oblong pieces of samosa pastry.

Preheat the oven to 220°C/425°F/Gas 7. Bring a small pan of water to the boil, add the diced potato, cover and cook for 10–15 minutes, until tender. Drain and set aside.

Meanwhile, heat the groundnut oil in a large frying pan and cook the shallots and garlic over a medium-heat, stirring occasionally, for 4–5 minutes, until softened and golden.

Add the drained diced potato, coconut milk, red or green curry paste, peas and lime juice to the frying pan. Mash together coarsely with a wooden spoon. Season to taste with salt and pepper and cook over a low heat for 2–3 minutes, then remove the pan from the heat and set aside until the mixture has cooled a little.

Lay a samosa wrapper or filo strip flat on the work surface. Brush with a little oil, then place a generous teaspoonful of the mixture in the middle of one end. Turn one corner diagonally over the filling to meet the long edge.

Continue folding over the filling, keeping the triangular shape as you work down the strip. Brush with a little more oil if necessary and place on a baking sheet. Prepare all the other samosas in the same way.

Bake for 15 minutes, or until the pastry is golden and crisp. Leave to cool slightly before serving.

Energy 56kcal/235kJ; Protein 1.3g; Carbohydrate 10g, of which sugars 0.8g; Fat 1.4g, of which saturates 0.2g; Cholesterol 0mg; Calcium 16mg; Fibre 0.7g; Sodium 8mg

HUMMUS

This classic Middle Eastern dish is made from cooked chickpeas, ground to a paste and flavoured with garlic, lemon juice, tahini, olive oil and cumin. It is delicious served with toasted pitta bread.

Serves 4–6

400g/14oz can chickpeas, drained
60ml/4 tbsp tahini
2–3 garlic cloves, chopped
juice of ½ –1 lemon
cayenne pepper
small pinch to 1.5ml/¼ tsp ground cumin, or more to taste
salt and ground black pepper

VARIATION
Process 2 roasted red (bell) peppers with the chickpeas, then continue as above. Serve sprinkled with lightly toasted pine nuts and paprika mixed with a little olive oil.

Energy 140kcal/1580kJ; Protein 6.9g; Carbohydrate 11.2g, of which sugars 0.4g; Fat 7.8g, of which saturates 1.1g; Cholesterol 0mg; Calcium 97mg; Fibre 3.6g; Sodium 149mg

Using a potato masher or food processor, coarsely mash the chickpeas. If you prefer a smoother purée, process them in a food processor or blender until smooth.

Mix the tahini into the chickpeas, then stir in the garlic, lemon juice, cayenne, cumin and salt and pepper to taste. If needed, add a little water. Serve at room temperature.

COOK'S TIP If using dried chickpeas soak them overnight, bring to the boil and then gently simmer for several hours until tender.

BABA GHANOUSH

The quantities in this richly flavoured dip can be varied according to taste. Adjust the amount of aubergine (eggplant), garlic and lemon juice depending on how creamy, garlicky or tart you prefer.

Serves 2–4

1 large or 2 medium aubergines (eggplant)
2–4 garlic cloves, chopped, to taste
90–150ml/6–10 tbsp tahini
juice of 1 lemon, or to taste
1.5ml/¼ tsp ground cumin, or to taste
salt
extra virgin olive oil, for drizzling
coriander (cilantro) leaves, hot pepper sauce and a few olives, to garnish
pitta bread or chunks of crusty French bread, to serve

Energy 91kcal/374kJ; Protein 1g;
Carbohydrate 2.2g, of which sugars 1.5g;
Fat 8.8g, of which saturates 1.4g;
Cholesterol 8mg; Calcium 8mg; Fibre 1,4g;
Sodium 52mg

Place the aubergine(s) directly over the flame of a gas stove. Turn them fairly frequently until deflated and the skin is evenly charred. Place them a plastic bag and seal tightly. Leave to cool.

Peel off the blackened skin from the aubergine(s), reserving the juices. Chop the flesh, put in a bowl and stir in the reserved juices.

Add the garlic and tahini to the aubergine and stir until smooth and well combined. Stir in the lemon juice. If the mixture becomes too thick, add 15–30ml/1–2 tbsp water or more lemon juice, if you like. Season with cumin and salt to taste.

Spoon the mixture into a serving bowl. Drizzle with olive oil and garnish with fresh coriander leaves, hot pepper sauce and olives.

GARLIC AND HERB BREAD

Excellent with soups or vegetable first courses, garlic bread is also irresistible just on its own. The better the bread, the better the final, garlicky version will be.

Serves 3–4
1 baguette or bloomer loaf

For the garlic and herb butter
*115g/4oz/½ cup unsalted
    butter, softened*
*5–6 large garlic cloves, finely
    chopped or crushed*
*30–45ml/2–3 tbsp chopped
    fresh herbs (such as parsley,
    chervil and a little tarragon)*
*15ml/1 tbsp snipped fresh
    chives*
*sea salt and ground black
    pepper*

> **VARIATION**
> Flavour the butter with
> garlic, chopped fresh chilli,
> and chopped coriander
> (cilantro).

Energy 920kcal/3877kJ; Protein 22.1g;
Carbohydrate 135.1g, of which sugars
7.2g; Fat 36.2g, of which saturates 20.8g;
Cholesterol 82mg; Calcium 317mg; Fibre
6.3g; Sodium 1714mg.

Preheat the oven to 200°C/400°F/Gas 6. Make the garlic and herb butter by beating the butter with the garlic, herbs, chives and seasoning.

Cut the bread into 1cm/½in thick diagonal slices, but leave them attached at the base so that the loaf stays intact.

Spread the butter between the slices, being careful not to detach them, and spread any remaining butter over the top of the loaf.

Wrap the loaf in foil and bake for 20–25 minutes, until the garlic and herb butter is melted and the crust is crisp. Cut into slices to serve.

HERB AND GARLIC TWISTS

These twists are very short and crumbly, made with garlic-flavoured dough sandwiched with fresh herbs and some chilli flakes for an extra kick. A very popular party nibble.

Makes about 20

90g/3½oz/scant ½ cup butter, at room temperature, diced
2 large garlic cloves, crushed
1 egg
1 egg yolk
175g/6oz/1½ cups self-raising (self-rising) flour
large pinch of salt
30ml/2 tbsp chopped fresh mixed herbs, such as basil, thyme, marjoram and flat leaf parsley
2.5–5ml/½–1 tsp dried chilli flakes
paprika or cayenne pepper, for sprinkling

Energy 71kcal/295kJ; Protein 1.4g;
Carbohydrate 6.9g, of which sugars 0.2g;
Fat 4.4g, of which saturates 2.5g;
Cholesterol 29mg; Calcium 19mg; Fibre
0.3g; Sodium 32mg

Preheat the oven to 200°C/400°F/Gas 6. Put the butter and garlic into a bowl and beat well. Add the egg and yolk and beat in thoroughly. Stir in the flour and salt and mix to a soft but not sticky dough.

Roll the dough out on a sheet of baking parchment to a 28cm/11in square. Using a sharp knife, cut it in half to make two rectangles.

Sprinkle the herbs and chilli flakes over one of the rectangles, then place the other rectangle on top. Gently roll the rolling pin over the herbs and chilli flakes to press them into the dough.

Using a sharp knife, cut the dough into 1cm/½in sticks. Make two twists in the centre of each one and place on a non-stick baking sheet.

Bake the twists for 15 minutes, or until crisp and golden brown. Cool on a wire rack. To serve, sprinkle with a little paprika or cayenne pepper.

FISH AND SHELLFISH

GARLIC, IN COMBINATION WITH OTHER
DELICIOUS INGREDIENTS SUCH AS SAFFRON,
FRESH HERBS, HOT SPICES, AND LEMON JUICE,
LENDS ITS DELIGHTFUL PUNGENCY TO FISH
SAUCES AND BAKES.

LANGOUSTINES WITH GARLIC BUTTER

There is nothing quite like the smell of garlic butter melting over shellfish. Freshly caught langoustines or jumbo shrimp are ideal for this simple yet extremely tasty first-course dish.

Serves 4

2 garlic cloves
5ml/1 tsp coarse salt
10ml/2 tsp chopped fresh flat leaf parsley, plus extra to garnish (optional)
250g/9oz/generous 1 cup butter, softened
juice of 2 lemons
pinch of cayenne pepper
20 freshly caught langoustines or Dublin Bay prawns (jumbo shrimp), cooked and peeled
ground black pepper

Energy 616kcal/2552kJ; Protein 29.7g; Carbohydrate 4.9g, of which sugars 0.6g; Fat 53.3g, of which saturates 33.1g; Cholesterol 192mg; Calcium 68mg; Fibre 0.5g; Sodium 1098mg.

Preheat the grill (broiler) to medium. Using a blender or food processor, blend the garlic cloves, salt and chopped parsley until quite well mixed. Then add the butter, lemon juice and cayenne pepper and blend again until all the ingredients are thoroughly combined.

Scrape the butter mixture out of the food processor and into a bowl.

Place the langoustines or prawns on a baking tray and put a blob of garlic butter on each one. Place under the preheated grill for about 5 minutes, or until the shellfish are cooked and the butter is bubbling.

Lift five shellfish on to each plate and spoon over the collected pan juices. Serve immediately with a grind or two of black pepper and garnished with chopped fresh flat leaf parsley if you like. Accompany with fresh bread for mopping up the juices.

GARLIC PRAWNS AND CHILLI

For this simple Spanish tapas dish, you really need fresh raw prawns (shrimp) which absorb the wonderful flavours of the garlic and chilli as they fry.

Serves 4
350–450g/12oz–1lb large
*   raw prawns (shrimp)*
2 red chillies
75ml/5 tbsp olive oil
3 garlic cloves, crushed
salt and ground black pepper

Remove the heads and shells from the prawns, leaving the tails intact.

Halve each chilli lengthways and discard the seeds. Heat the oil in a flameproof pan, suitable for serving. (Alternatively, use a frying pan and have a warmed serving dish ready in the oven.)

Add all the prawns, chilli and garlic to the pan and cook over a high heat for about 3 minutes, stirring until the prawns turn pink. Season lightly with salt and pepper and serve immediately.

Serve with warm bread.

COOK'S TIP
Have everything ready for last-minute cooking so you can take it to the table while it is still sizzling.

Energy 118kcal/495kJ; Protein 17.9g; Carbohydrate 3g, of which sugars 3g; Fat 3.9g, of which saturates 0.5g; Cholesterol 195mg; Calcium 83mg; Fibre 0.4g; Sodium 234mg.

GARLIC-STUFFED MUSSELS

This recipe hails from Ireland where wild herbs, including garlic, have been used for hundreds of years. Serve with plenty of crusty bread to mop up the juices.

Serves 4–6

2kg/4½lb fresh mussels
175g/6oz/¾ cup butter
4–6 garlic cloves
50g/2oz/1 cup fresh white breadcrumbs
15ml/1 tbsp chopped fresh parsley
juice of 1 lemon
brown bread, to serve

Wash the mussels in cold water. Remove the beards and discard any with broken shells, or those that don't close when tapped.

Put the mussels into a shallow, heavy pan, without adding any liquid. Cover tightly and cook over a high heat for a few minutes, until all the mussels have opened. Discard any that fail to open.

Remove the top shell from each mussel and arrange the bottom shells with the mussels in a shallow flameproof dish.

Melt the butter in a small pan, add the crushed garlic, breadcrumbs, parsley and lemon juice. Mix well and sprinkle this mixture over the mussels.

Cook under a hot grill (broiler) until golden brown. Serve very hot, with freshly baked brown bread.

COOK'S TIP
A glass of stout, such as Guinness, Beamish or Murphy's, goes down very well with these mussels.

Energy 500Kcal/2082kJ; Protein 27.7g; Carbohydrate 10g, of which sugars 0.6g; Fat 39.2g, of which saturates 23.3g; Cholesterol 153mg; Calcium 319mg; Fibre 0.3g; Sodium 675mg

BAKED TROUT WITH GARLIC BUTTER

In this delicious recipe whole trout are simply baked in the oven, drizzled with hot garlic butter and served with sprigs of parsley and wedges of lemon.

Serves 4

2 garlic cloves, crushed
50g/2oz/¼ cup butter, softened, plus extra, for greasing
4 medium-sized trout, about 300g/11oz each, cleaned and gutted
45ml/3 tbsp lemon juice
salt and ground black pepper, to taste
lemon wedges and fresh parsley sprigs, to garnish

Mix together the garlic and butter in a bowl. Set aside until required.

Preheat the oven to 200°C/400°F/Gas 6. Grease a large baking dish.

Place the fish in the baking dish. Pour the lemon juice all over and inside the trout, then season with salt and pepper and put in the oven.

Bake the trout for 15–20 minutes, or until the flesh flakes easily when you insert the point of a sharp knife. Place on warm serving plates.

Melt the garlic butter in a pan, then pour over the fish. Garnish with lemon and parsley, and serve immediately.

Energy 205kcal/853kJ; Protein 19.5g; Carbohydrate 0.1g, of which sugars 0.1g; Fat 14.1g, of which saturates 6.5g; Cholesterol 27mg; Calcium 11mg; Fibre 0g; Sodium 132mg.

COOK'S TIP
If fresh trout is not available use salmon instead.

BOUILLABAISSE

Authentic bouillabaisse comes from the south of France. Suitable fish for this dish include rascasse, conger eel, monkfish, red gurnard and John Dory. Use as large a variety of fish as you can.

Serves 4

45ml/3 tbsp olive oil
2 onions, chopped
2 leeks, white parts only,
chopped
4 garlic cloves, chopped
450g/1lb ripe tomatoes, peeled
and chopped
3 litres/5 pints/12 cups boiling
fish stock or water
15ml/1 tbsp tomato purée
(paste)
large pinch of saffron threads
1 fresh bouquet garni,
containing 2 thyme sprigs, 2
bay leaves and 2 fennel sprigs
3kg/6½ lb mixed fish, cleaned
and cut into large chunks
4 potatoes, peeled and sliced
salt, pepper and cayenne
pepper

For the garnish

slices of French bread, toasted
and rubbed with garlic
30ml/2 tbsp chopped fresh
parsley

Heat the oil in a large pan. Add the onions, leeks, garlic and tomatoes. Cook until slightly softened. Stir in the stock or water, tomato purée and saffron. Add the bouquet garni and boil until the oil is amalgamated. Lower the heat; add the fish and potatoes.

Simmer the soup for 5–8 minutes, removing each type of fish as it becomes cooked. Continue to cook until the potatoes are very tender. Season well with salt, pepper and cayenne.

Divide the fish and potatoes among individual soup plates. Strain the soup and ladle it over the fish. Garnish with toasted French bread and parsley.

Energy 322kcal/1344kJ; Protein 46.8g; Carbohydrate 3.2g, of which sugars 2.8g; Fat 13.1g, of which saturates 1.9g; Cholesterol 115mg; Calcium 38mg; Fibre 1.3g; Sodium 163mg.

MEAT AND POULTRY

WHETHER USED DISCREETLY WITH ROASTED

QUAIL OR A SHOULDER OF LAMB, OR BOLDLY AND

ABUNDANTLY IN A CLASSIC CHICKEN DISH,

GARLIC ADDS WONDERFUL FLAVOUR TO ALL

KINDS OF MEAT AND POULTRY RECIPES.

CHICKEN WINGS WITH GARLIC AND SUMAC

The aroma of chicken wings or drumsticks grilling over charcoal is always enticing, whether it is in a busy street market or in a clearing in the countryside.

Serves 4–6
45–60ml/3–4 tbsp olive oil
juice of 1 lemon
4 cloves garlic, crushed
15ml/1 tbsp ground sumac
16–20 chicken wings
sea salt

COOK'S TIP
These tasty chicken wings are perfect for a picnic. Eat with your fingers straight from the barbecue.

Energy 272kcal/1132kJ; Protein 23g;
Carbohydrate 1.4g, of which sugars 0.1g;
Fat 19.5g, of which saturates 4.7g;
Cholesterol 98mg; Calcium 12mg; Fibre
0.1g; Sodium 68mg

In a bowl, mix together the olive oil, lemon juice, crushed garlic and sumac. Place the chicken wings in a shallow dish and rub the marinade all over them. Cover the dish and leave to marinate in the refrigerator for 2 hours.

Prepare the barbecue or preheat a conventional grill (broiler). Place the chicken wings on the rack and cook for about 3 minutes on each side, basting them with the marinade while they cook. Alternatively, preheat the oven to 180°C/350°F/Gas 4, place the chicken wings in an ovenproof dish, brush liberally with the marinade and roast for 25–30 minutes.

When the wings are completely cooked, remove from the heat, sprinkle with salt and serve while still hot.

CHICKEN WITH FORTY CLOVES OF GARLIC

This dish does not have to be mathematically exact, so do not worry if you have 35 or even 50 cloves of garlic – the important thing is that there should be lots.

Serves 4–5

5–6 whole heads of garlic
15g/½oz/1 tbsp butter
45ml/3 tbsp olive oil
1.8–2kg/4–4½lb chicken
150g/5oz/1¼ cups plain (all-purpose) flour, plus 5ml/1 tsp
75ml/5 tbsp white port, Pineau de Charentes or other white, fortified wine
2–3 fresh tarragon or rosemary sprigs
30ml/2 tbsp crème fraîche (optional)
few drops of lemon juice (optional)
salt and ground black pepper

Separate 3 of the heads of garlic into cloves and peel them. Remove the first layer of papery skin from the remaining heads of garlic and cut off the tops to expose the cloves, if you like, or leave them whole. Preheat the oven to 180°C/350°F/Gas 4.

Heat the butter and 15ml/1 tbsp of the olive oil in a flameproof casserole that is just large enough to take the chicken and garlic. Add the chicken and cook over a medium heat, turning frequently, for 10–15 minutes, until it is browned all over.

Sprinkle in 5ml/1 tsp flour and cook for 1 minute. Add the port or wine. Tuck in the whole heads of garlic and the peeled cloves with the herb sprigs. Pour over the remaining oil and season to taste with salt and pepper.

Mix the main batch of flour with sufficient water to make a firm dough. Roll it out into a long sausage and press it around the rim of the casserole, then press on the lid, folding the dough up and over it to create a tight seal. Cook in the oven for 1½ hours.

To serve, lift off the lid to break the seal and remove the chicken and whole garlic to a serving platter and keep warm. Remove and discard the herb sprigs, then place the casserole on the hob and whisk to combine the garlic cloves with the juices. Add the crème fraîche, if using, and a little lemon juice to taste. Process the sauce in a food processor or blender or press through a sieve if a smoother result is required. Serve the garlic purée with the chicken.

Energy 616kcal/2565kJ; Protein 37.7g; Carbohydrate 31.6g, of which sugars 2.9g; Fat 36.5g, of which saturates 10.4g; Cholesterol 173mg; Calcium 64mg; Fibre 2.6g; Sodium 151mg

GARLIC-ROASTED QUAILS WITH HONEY

This is a great Indo-Chinese favourite made with quails or poussins. Crispy, tender and juicy, they are simple to prepare and delicious to eat. Roast them in the oven or over a barbecue.

Serves 4

150ml/¼ pint/⅔ cup
    mushroom soy sauce
45ml/3 tbsp honey
15ml/1 tbsp sugar
8 garlic cloves, crushed
15ml/1 tbsp black peppercorns,
    crushed
30ml/2 tbsp sesame oil
8 quails or poussins
nuoc cham, *to serve*

In a bowl, beat the mushroom soy sauce with the honey and sugar until the sugar has dissolved. Stir in the garlic, crushed peppercorns and sesame oil. Put the quails or poussins into a dish and rub the marinade over them with your fingers. Cover and chill for at least 4 hours.

Preheat the oven to 230°C/450°F/Gas 8. Place the quails breast side down in a roasting pan or on a wire rack set over a baking tray, then put them in the oven for 10 minutes.

Take them out and turn them over so they are breast side up, baste well with the juices and return them to the oven for a further 15–20 minutes. Serve immediately with nuoc cham for dipping or drizzling over the meat.

Energy 649Kcal/2701kJ; Protein 51g; Carbohydrate 17g, of which sugars 3g; Fat 43g, of which saturates 11g; Cholesterol 250mg; Calcium 61mg; Fibre 0.2g; Sodium 0.2g

COOK'S TIP

If you can't find quails or poussins for this dish, you could easily improvise by making it with whole chicken legs instead. The results will be just as good, and the cooking times similar.

CURRIED PORK WITH PICKLED GARLIC

This very rich curry is best accompanied by lots of plain rice and perhaps a light vegetable dish. It could serve four if served with a vegetable curry. Asian stores sell pickled garlic.

Serves 2

130g/4½oz lean pork steaks
30ml/2 tbsp vegetable oil
1 garlic clove, crushed
15ml/1 tbsp Thai red curry paste
130ml/4½fl oz/generous ½ cup
  coconut cream
2.5cm/1in piece fresh root
  ginger, finely chopped
30ml/2 tbsp vegetable or
  chicken stock
30ml/2 tbsp Thai fish sauce
5ml/1 tsp granulated sugar
2.5ml/½ tsp ground turmeric
10ml/2 tsp lemon juice
4 pickled garlic cloves, finely
  chopped
strips of lemon and lime rind,
  to garnish

Place the pork steaks in the freezer for 30–40 minutes, until firm, then, using a sharp knife, cut the meat into fine slivers, trimming off any excess fat.

Heat the oil in a wok or large, heavy frying pan and cook the garlic over a low to medium heat until golden brown. Do not let it burn. Add the curry paste and stir it in well.

Add the coconut cream and stir until the liquid begins to reduce and thicken. Stir in the pork. Cook for 2 minutes more, until the pork is cooked through.

Add the ginger, stock, fish sauce, sugar and turmeric, stirring constantly, then add the lemon juice and pickled garlic. Spoon into bowls, garnish with strips of rind, and serve.

Energy 227kcal/947kJ; Protein 16.3g; Carbohydrate 9.8g, of which sugars 6.1g; Fat 14g, of which saturates 2.4g; Cholesterol 41mg; Calcium 30mg; Fibre 1g; Sodium 474mg.

ROAST SHOULDER OF LAMB WITH WHOLE GARLIC CLOVES

The potatoes catch the lamb fat as it cooks, giving garlicky, juicy results. Return the potatoes to the oven to keep warm while you leave the lamb to rest before carving. Serve with seasonal vegetables.

Serves 4–6

675g/1½lb waxy potatoes,
*   peeled and cut into large dice*
12 garlic cloves, unpeeled
1 whole shoulder of lamb
45ml/3 tbsp olive oil
salt and ground black pepper

Preheat the oven to 180°C/350°F/Gas 4. Put the potatoes and garlic cloves into a large roasting pan and season with salt and pepper. Pour over 30ml/2 tbsp of the oil and toss the potatoes and garlic to coat.

Place a rack over the roasting pan, so that it is not touching the potatoes. Place the lamb on the rack and drizzle over the remaining oil. Season with salt and pepper.

Roast the lamb and potatoes for 2–2½ hours, or until the lamb is cooked through. Halfway through the cooking time, carefully take the lamb and the rack off the roasting pan and turn the potatoes to ensure even cooking.

Energy 668kcal/2775kJ; Protein 29.2g; Carbohydrate 20.8g, of which sugars 1.7g; Fat 52.6g, of which saturates 24.1g; Cholesterol 113mg; Calcium 22mg; Fibre 1.8g; Sodium 123mg.

ROAST FILLET OF BEEF WITH WILD GARLIC HOLLANDAISE

Fillet steak is magnificent when cooked to perfection and served with a luxurious sauce. The aroma of wild garlic is unmistakable and can be smelt from a distance – very garlicky.

Serves 4

4 fillet steaks (beef tenderloin)
15ml/1 tbsp olive oil
5ml/1 tsp butter
15ml/1 tbsp dry white wine
2 egg yolks
250g/9oz/generous 1 cup
  butter, melted
20 wild garlic leaves
squeeze of lemon juice
  (optional)
salt and ground black pepper

VARIATION

If you are finding it hard to get fresh wild garlic, or it is out of season, you can use a garlic clove instead, chopped finely and added at the end in the same way as the leaves.

Energy 744kcal/3076kJ; Protein 33.8g;
Carbohydrate 0.6g, of which sugars 0.6g;
Fat 67.1g, of which saturates 38.6g;
Cholesterol 328mg; Calcium 42mg; Fibre
0.3g; Sodium 459mg.

Dry the steaks using kitchen paper and set aside.

Heat a heavy pan and add the oil and butter. Just as the butter is starting to bubble up, place the steaks in the pan. Keep the pan hot and brown the steaks all over to seal in the juices, then reduce the heat to cook the meat to whatever stage of pinkness you want; 6 minutes will make them medium rare.

Remove the steaks from the pan and keep warm between two plates.

Allow the pan to cool for a few minutes then pour in the wine. If it bubbles up as you pour it in, wait for the pan to cool a little more before pouring in the rest.

Whisk the egg yolks until smooth and blended, then whisk them into the wine over a low heat, taking care that they don't scramble. They should foam and thicken slightly. Remove them from the heat if they begin to firm up.

Then, off the heat, slowly pour in the melted butter, a little bit to start with, whisking all the time. (You may not wish to add all the whey from the butter as it tends to make the sauce less thick.) This is where the handle comes in, and putting the pan on a damp cloth will help to stop it from moving about.

Rinse the wild garlic leaves thoroughly and drain on kitchen paper. Shred them finely and stir gently into the hollandaise. Season to taste with salt and ground black pepper. If you want a sharper taste, add a squeeze or two of fresh lemon juice.

Using prewarmed plates, place one steak on each, in the centre. Then spoon the wild garlic hollandaise over the top, letting it spill over on to the side of the plate. Serve with roast potatoes and lightly steamed vegetables.

VEGETARIAN AND SIDE DISHES

A COMBINATION OF SIMPLE INGREDIENTS
ROBUSTLY SEASONED WITH GARLIC ADDS UP
TO FABULOUS FLAVOUR IN AN EXCITING
COLLECTION OF DISHES, INCLUDING PASTA,
RICE, EGGS AND STUFFED MUSHROOMS

SPAGHETTI WITH GARLIC AND OIL

In Italy this dish is sometimes given its full name of Spaghetti Aglio, Olio e Peperoncino *because chilli –* peperoncino *– is always included to give the dish some bite.*

Serves 4

400g/14oz fresh or dried spaghetti
90ml/6 tbsp extra virgin olive oil
2–4 garlic cloves, crushed
1 dried red chilli
1 small handful fresh flat leaf (Italian) parsley, roughly chopped
salt

Cook the pasta according to the packet instructions, adding plenty of salt to the water.

Meanwhile, heat the oil very gently in a frying pan. Add the crushed garlic and whole dried chilli and stir over a low heat until the garlic is just beginning to brown. Remove the chilli and keep for the garnish.

Drain the pasta and transfer it into a warmed large bowl. Pour on the oil and garlic mixture, add the parsley and toss vigorously until the pasta glistens. Serve immediately. Add the chilli as a garnish, if you like.

COOK'S TIPS

• Since the oil is such an important ingredient here, only use the very best cold-pressed extra virgin olive oil.

• Don't use salt in the oil and garlic mixture, because it will not dissolve sufficiently.

Energy 505kcal/2126kJ; Protein 12.8g; Carbohydrate 76.4g, of which sugars 3.5g; Fat 18.6g, of which saturates 2.6g; Cholesterol 0mg; Calcium 27mg; Fibre 3.3g; Sodium 3mg

FRENCH RAREBIT WITH SHALLOT AND GARLIC CONFIT

The inspiration for this recipe comes from Switzerland, the home of cheese fondue and raclette (melted cheese). If you can imagine grilled fondue on toast, then this is it.

Serves 4

25g/1oz/2 tbsp butter
5ml/1 tsp Dijon mustard
30ml/2 tbsp medium to sweet white wine
75g/3oz Gruyère or raclette cheese, grated
pinch of cayenne pepper
2 long thick slices crusty French baguette, cut on the slant
2 egg yolks

For the confit

75ml/5 tbsp olive oil
675g/1½lb shallots, quartered
675g/1½lb red onions, finely sliced
4 garlic cloves, thinly sliced (preferably smoked garlic)
120ml/4fl oz/½ cup sherry vinegar or half dry sherry and half balsamic vinegar
30ml/2 tbsp crème de cassis
salt and ground black pepper

To make the confit, heat the oil in a large pan over a medium heat. Add the shallots, sliced onions and garlic, stirring to coat with the oil. (Use smoked garlic if you can get it as the lovely smoky and nutty flavour really comes through the sweetness of the confit to add an earthiness to the whole dish.) Add just a couple of tablespoons of water and put on the lid. Cook slowly for 20 minutes, without lifting the lid, to steam and soften the onions.

Uncover the pan, stir well and continue to cook very slowly for about 1 hour until the onions are very soft and caramelized.

Stir the vinegar and cassis into the pan and season with salt and pepper. Cook for about 10 minutes more, to evaporate the vinegar. The confit should look thick and sticky. Leave to cool, then carefully spoon into a preserving jar, cover with a layer of olive oil and keep in the refrigerator.

To make the rarebit, preheat the grill (broiler). Put the butter, mustard, white wine, cheese and cayenne pepper in a small pan and slowly melt over a gentle heat. Set aside for a moment.

Toast the slices of baguette on one side. Beat the egg yolk into the melted cheese and spread over the un-toasted side of the bread.

Put under the grill for 2–3 minutes until browned and bubbling. Serve with a good dollop of the sweet onion and garlic confit.

Energy 513kcal/2132kJ; Protein 12g; Carbohydrate 38g, of which sugars 13g; Fat 34g, of which saturates 11g; Cholesterol 133mg; Calcium 281mg; Fibre 4.4g; Sodium 541mg

STUFFED MUSHROOMS BAKED IN GARLIC BREADCRUMBS

Serve these succulent Stilton-stuffed mushrooms with chunks of warm, crusty bread or fresh rolls to soak up all their delicious garlic-flavoured juices.

Serves 4

450g/1lb chestnut mushrooms
3 garlic cloves, finely chopped
90g/3½oz/7 tbsp butter,
  melted
juice of ½ lemon
115g/4oz Stilton cheese,
  crumbled
50g/2oz/½ cup walnuts,
  chopped
90g/3½oz/1 cup fresh
  white breadcrumbs
25g/1oz Parmesan cheese,
  grated
30ml/2 tbsp chopped fresh
  parsley
salt and ground black pepper

COOK'S TIP
A simple sauce of fromage frais or thick Greek yogurt with some chopped fresh herbs and a little Dijon mustard stirred through goes well with these tasty mushrooms.

Preheat the oven to 200°C/400°F/Gas 6. Place the mushrooms in an ovenproof dish and scatter half the garlic over them. Drizzle with 60ml/4 tbsp of the butter and the lemon juice. Season with salt and pepper and bake for 15–20 minutes. Leave to cool.

Cream the crumbled Stilton with the chopped walnuts and mix in 30ml/2 tbsp of the breadcrumbs.

Remove the mushroom stacks and stuff the mushrooms with the cheese mixture.

Preheat the grill (broiler). Mix the remaining garlic, breadcrumbs and melted butter together. Stir in the Parmesan and parsley and season with pepper. Top the mushrooms with the breadcrumb mixture and grill (broil) for 5 minutes until crisp and browned. Serve at once.

EGGS WITH GARLIC AND SUMAC

This dish is very popular in the streets and at bus and train stations in Turkey, and is occasionally served with garlic-flavoured yogurt, a great favourite of the Turks, or a tahini or nut sauce.

Serves 3–4
6 free-range eggs
30ml/2 tbsp olive oil
a knob (pat) of butter
2–3 cloves garlic, crushed
5–10ml/1–2 tsp dried sumac
5ml/1 tsp dried mint
sea salt
garlic-spiced yogurt, to serve

Crack all the eggs into a large bowl, being very careful not to break any of the yolks as you do so.

Heat the oil in a heavy frying pan with the butter. Stir in the garlic and sumac and fry for 2–3 minutes.

Slip the eggs into the pan, moving the bowl so that each one falls into its own section of the pan.

Sprinkle the dried mint over the eggs and cover the pan with a lid. Reduce the heat and cook until the egg yolks are set to taste.

Sprinkle a little sea salt over the eggs and divide them into portions. Serve immediately with garlic-spiced yogurt and an extra pinch of sumac if you like.

Energy 220kcal/911kJ; Protein 12g; Carbohydrate 0g; Fat 20g, of which saturates 5g; Cholesterol 362mg; Calcium 65mg; Fibre 0.1 g; Sodium 243mg.

COOK'S TIP
To make garlic-spiced yogurt mash two garlic cloves with a little salt and mix well with thick yogurt.

POTATO, ONION AND GARLIC GRATIN

This tasty side dish makes the perfect accompaniment to family roasts and stews. Cooking the potatoes in stock with onions and garlic gives them a really rich flavour.

Serves 4

40g/1½oz/3 tbsp butter
1 large onion, finely sliced into rings
2–4 garlic cloves, finely chopped
2.5ml/½ tsp dried thyme
900g/2lb waxy potatoes, very finely sliced
450ml/¾ pint/scant 2 cups boiling vegetable stock
sea salt and ground black pepper

> **VARIATIONS**
> To vary the flavour, try using chopped rosemary or sage in place of the thyme, or use crushed juniper berries instead.

Energy 260Kcal/1092kJ; Protein 5.1g; Carbohydrate 41.9g, of which sugars 6.4g; Fat 9.1g, of which saturates 5.4g; Cholesterol 21mg; Calcium 31mg; Fibre 3.3g; Sodium 171mg.

Preheat the oven to 200°C/375°F/Gas 5. Grease the inside of a shallow ceramic baking dish with 15g/½oz/1 tbsp of the butter.

Spoon a thin layer of onions on to the base of the dish, then sprinkle over a little of the chopped garlic, thyme, salt and pepper.

Carefully arrange an overlapping layer of potato slices on top of the onion mixture in the dish. Continue to layer the ingredients until all the onions, garlic, herbs and potatoes are used up, finishing with a layer of sliced potatoes.

Pour just enough of the stock into the dish to cover the potatoes. Cover tightly with foil and bake in the oven for 1 hour until the potatoes are tender.

At the end of the cooking time remove the foil and brown the potatoes in the oven for 3–4 minutes. Serve sprinkled with a little salt and ground black pepper.

GARLIC AND GINGER RICE WITH CORIANDER

In Vietnam, when rice is served on the side, it is usually steamed and plain, or fragrant with the flavours of garlic, ginger and herbs. It compliments almost any vegetable, fish or meat dish.

Serves 4–6

15ml/1 tbsp vegetable or groundnut (peanut) oil
2–3 garlic cloves, finely chopped
25g/1oz fresh root ginger, finely chopped
225g/8oz/generous 1 cup long grain rice, rinsed in several bowls of water and drained
900ml/1½ pints/3¾ cups vegetable stock
a bunch of fresh coriander (cilantro) leaves, finely chopped

Heat the oil in a clay pot or heavy pan. Stir in the garlic and ginger and fry until golden. Stir in the rice and allow it to absorb the flavours for 1–2 minutes. Pour in the stock and stir to make sure the rice doesn't stick. Bring the stock to the boil, then reduce the heat.

Scatter the coriander over the surface of the stock, cover the pan, and leave to cook gently for 20–25 minutes, until the rice has absorbed all the liquid. Turn off the heat and gently fluff up the rice to mix in the coriander. Cover and leave to infuse for 10 minutes before serving.

Energy 151Kcal/632kJ; Protein 3g; Carbohydrate 30g, of which sugars 0g; Fat 2g, of which saturates 0.3g; Cholesterol 0mg; Calcium 9mg; Fibre 0.1g; Sodium 124mg

GREEN BEANS WITH GARLIC

Delicate and fresh-tasting flageolet beans and garlic add a distinct French flavour to this simple side dish. It can accompany many roast dishes.

SERVES 4

225g/8oz flageolet (or
  cannellini) beans
15ml/1 tbsp olive oil
25g/1oz/2 tbsp butter
1 onion, finely chopped
1–2 garlic cloves, crushed
3–4 tomatoes, peeled and
  chopped
350g/12oz runner (green)
  beans, prepared and sliced
150ml/¼ pint/⅔ cup white
  wine
150ml/¼ pint/⅔ cup vegetable
  stock
30ml/2 tbsp chopped fresh
  parsley
salt and freshly ground black
  pepper

Energy 248kcal/1040kJ; Protein 13g;
Carbohydrate 23g, of which sugars 23g; Fat
17g, of which saturates 5g; Cholesterol
13mg; Calcium 236mg; Fibre 20g; Sodium
88mg.

Place the flageolet beans in a large pan of water, bring to the boil and simmer for ¾–1 hour until tender. Drain well in a colander or sieve (strainer).

Heat the oil and butter in a large frying pan and sauté the onion and garlic for 3–4 minutes until soft. Add the chopped tomatoes and continue cooking over a gentle heat until they are soft.

Stir the flageolet beans into the onion and tomato mixture, then add the green beans, wine, stock, and a little salt. Stir well. Cover and simmer for 5–10 minutes until the beans are tender.

Increase the heat to reduce the liquid, then stir in the parsley and season with a little more salt, if necessary, and pepper.

ROASTED BEETROOT WITH GARLIC SAUCE

The combination of the concentrated sweetness of the beetroot (beets) with the sharpness of the garlic sauce is truly irresistible. Serve with warm crusty bread to mop up the juices.

Serves 4

675g/1½lb medium or small beetroot (beets)

75–90ml/5–6 tbsp extra virgin olive oil

For the garlic sauce

4 medium slices of bread, crusts removed, soaked in water for 10 minutes

2–3 garlic cloves, chopped

15ml/1 tbsp white wine vinegar

60ml/4 tbsp extra virgin olive oil

salt

Preheat the oven to 180°C/350°F/Gas 4. Rinse the beetroot to remove any grit, place in foil and drizzle a little oil over them and seal the foil. Bake for about 1½ hours until perfectly soft.

To make the garlic sauce, squeeze most of the water out of the bread, but leave it quite moist. Place it in a blender or food processor. Add the garlic and vinegar, with salt to taste, and blend until smooth.

While the blender or processor is running, drizzle in the olive oil through the lid or feeder tube. The sauce should be runny. Spoon it into a bowl and set it aside.

Remove the beetroot from the foil. When they are cool enough to handle, peel them. Slice them in thin round slices and arrange on a flat platter. Drizzle the remaining oil all over and serve with the sauce.

Energy 344kcal/1435kJ; Protein 5.1g; Carbohydrate 25.7g, of which sugars 12.5g; Fat 25.4g, of which saturates 3.6g; Cholesterol 0mg; Calcium 62mg; Fibre 3.6g; Sodium 247mg.

SHALLOT AND GARLIC TARTE TATIN

Savoury versions of the famous apple tarte Tatin have been popular for years. Here, shallots are caramelized in butter, sugar and vinegar before being baked beneath a layer of Parmesan pastry.

Serves 4–6

300g/11oz puff pastry, thawed if frozen
50g/2oz/¼ cup butter
75g/3oz/1 cup freshly grated Parmesan cheese
40g/1½oz/3 tbsp butter
500g/1¼lb shallots
12–16 large garlic cloves, peeled but left whole
15ml/1 tbsp golden caster sugar
15ml/1 tbsp balsamic or sherry vinegar
45ml/3 tbsp water
5ml/1 tsp chopped fresh thyme, plus a few extra sprigs (optional)
salt and ground black pepper

Roll out the pastry into a rectangle. Spread the butter over it, leaving a 2.5cm/1in border. Scatter the Parmesan on top. Fold the bottom third of the pastry up to cover the middle and the top third down. Seal the edges, give a quarter turn and roll out to a rectangle, then fold as before. Chill for 30 minutes.

Melt the butter in a 23–25cm/9–10in round heavy tin or skillet that will go in the oven. Add the shallots and garlic, and cook until lightly browned all over.

Scatter the sugar over the top and increase the heat a little. Cook until the sugar begins to caramelize, then turn the shallots and garlic in the buttery juices. Add the vinegar, water, thyme and seasoning. Cook, part-covered, for 5–8 minutes, until the garlic cloves are just tender. Cool.

Preheat the oven to 190°C/375°F/Gas 5. Roll out the pastry to the diameter of the tin or skillet and lay it over the shallots and garlic. Prick the pastry with a sharp knife, then bake for 25–35 minutes, or until the pastry is risen and golden. Set aside to cool for 5–10 minutes, then invert the tart on to a serving platter. Scatter with a few thyme sprigs, if you like, and serve

Energy 618kcal/2567kJ; Protein 12.8g; Carbohydrate 35.5g, of which sugars 9.6g; Fat 48.2g, of which saturates 22.8g; Cholesterol 79mg; Calcium 313mg; Fibre 3g; Sodium 605mg.

PISSALADIÈRE

This famous onion and anchovy dish is a traditional market food of Nice in southern France. It can be made using either shortcrust pastry or, as here, yeasted dough, similar to a pizza base.

Serves 6

250g/9oz/2¼ cups strong plain (all-purpose) flour, plus extra for dusting
50g/2oz/⅓ cup fine polenta
5ml/1 tsp salt
175ml/6fl oz/¾ cup lukewarm water
5ml/1 tsp dried yeast
5ml/1 tsp caster sugar
30ml/2 tbsp extra virgin olive oil

For the topping

60–75ml/4–5 tbsp extra virgin olive oil
6 large sweet Spanish onions, thinly sliced
2 large garlic cloves, thinly sliced
5ml/1 tsp chopped fresh thyme, plus several sprigs
1 fresh rosemary sprig
1–2 x 50g/2oz cans anchovies in olive oil
50–75g/2–3oz small black olives
salt and ground black pepper

Mix the flour, polenta and salt in a large mixing bowl. Pour half the water into a bowl. Add the yeast and sugar, then leave in a warm place for 10 minutes, until frothy. Pour the yeast mixture into the flour mixture with the remaining water and the olive oil.

Using your hands, mix all the ingredients together to form a dough, then turn out and knead for 5 minutes, until smooth, springy and elastic.

Return the dough to the clean, floured bowl and place it in a plastic bag or cover with oiled clear film (plastic wrap), then set the dough aside for 30–60 minutes to rise and double in bulk.

Meanwhile, start to prepare the topping. Heat 45ml/3 tbsp of the olive oil in a large, heavy-based saucepan and add the sliced onions. Stir well to coat the onions in the oil, then cover the pan and cook over a very low heat, stirring occasionally, for 20-30 minutes.

Add a little salt to taste and the garlic, thyme and rosemary. Stir well and continue cooking for another 15–25 minutes, or until the onions are soft and deep golden yellow but not browned at all. Uncover the pan for the last 5–10 minutes' cooking if the onions seem very wet. Remove and discard the rosemary. Set the onions aside to cool.

Preheat the oven to 220°C/425°F/Gas 7. Roll out the dough thinly and use to line a large baking sheet, about 30 x 23–25cm/12 x 9–10in.

Drain the anchovies, cut them in half lengthways and arrange them in a lattice pattern over the onions. Scatter the olives and thyme sprigs over the top of the pissaladière and drizzle with the remaining olive oil. Bake for about 20–25 minutes. Season with pepper and serve warm.

Energy 436kcal/1815kJ; Protein 5.9g; Carbohydrate 37.4g, of which sugars 5.8g; Fat 31.1g, of which saturates 1.5g; Cholesterol 0mg; Calcium 77mg; Fibre 1.5g; Sodium 542mg.

INDEX

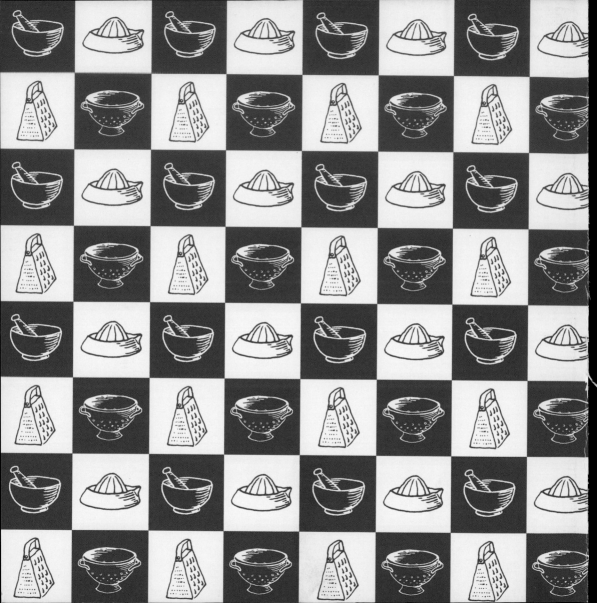